Smashing Myths
Understanding Madison's Notes on Nullification

MICHAEL MAHARREY

ISBN: 0615925340
ISBN-13: 978-0615925349

DEDICATION

This book is dedicated to my mother, Sharon Norris. She taught me to think for myself and instilled in me the value of hard work.

CONTENTS

ACKNOWLEDGMENTS

As with any project, this little book was a team effort.

Thanks to Michael Boldin for making it possible. This book is the result of many hours of back and forth, and spirited discussion. His name should probably be on the front cover too.

Michael Lotfi, William Kennedy and Mitchell Toland Jr. each provided valuable editing assistance.

And a special thanks to my wife Cynthia Maharrey. Nothing I do would be possible without her support help and encouragement.

1 INTRODUCTION

Opponents of nullification like to use James Madison's 1835 *Notes on Nullification* to create a kind of a "gotcha" moment.

The Madison-penned *Virginia Resolutions of 1798*, along with his *Virginia Report of 1800,* serve as two foundational documents in understanding the principles of nullification. But nullification-deniers use the *Notes* to argue Madison didn't mean what he appeared to have said in 1798. They go so far as to claim that Madison never even supported the idea of nullification. They gleefully point to particular passages in the *Notes* and declare, "Aha! See! Madison opposed nullification."

So, what gives?

Have nullifiers misconstrued Madison's earlier writings? Was he always opposed to state nullification? Did he do a complete 180 later in life? Or, do the opponents of nullification misconstrue his 1835 *Notes*?

Understanding Madison's *Notes on Nullification* requires careful attention to the entire document. Pulling single quotes, or even longer passages, out of context can easily lead to a misunderstanding of what Madison meant. In fact, grasping Madison's nuanced argument requires understanding the terms he used and the context of the document as a whole.

Context provides the key, and when interpreting any writing, the reader must always consider contextual clues. When it comes to Madison's *Notes*, there are three important areas to understand in order to get it right.

First, we have context within a document itself. People tend to feature single quotes from a given text to make their point, but oftentimes ignore information that places their favored passage in a different light. Nullification opponents find quotes in the *Notes* that seem to support their assertion that Madison did not favor state nullification. But a close reading of the entire document also finds Madison specifically defending nullification.

Solid textual interpretation demands that we don't simply disregard information contrary to our position, but find a way to reconcile seemingly contradictory statements.

Second, we have to place the document in the context of the writer's other work. When ideas from one source seem to contradict those expressed by the author in other works, the reader can't simply ignore the inconsistency and pick the idea closest to one's own views.

We have to make some effort to reconcile the differing points of view. Did the author change his mind? Is he simply just an inconsistent thinker? Or did we miss clues that actually reconcile apparent discrepancies?

Finally, we have to understand the historical context surrounding the document's writing. What was going on at the time? How did the current situation impact the writer's thinking? And perhaps most importantly, what specifically was he addressing?

By closely examining Madison's *Notes on Nullification* through these contextual lenses, we find he was addressing a very specific situation and never renounced the basic tenants of nullification as the modern movement defines it.

2 HISTORICAL CONTEXT

In 1828, Congress passed a tariff designed to protect the northern industrial economy, struggling to compete against low cost imported goods. Southerners generally opposed the tariff because it raised the price of goods imported into southern states. It also indirectly hurt the southern agrarian economy by reducing cash available for the English to purchase southern cotton. Opposition proved particularly fierce in South Carolina. Many southerners dubbed it the Tariff of Abominations.

Opponents claimed the tariff of 1828 was unconstitutional because it benefited only certain sections of the country to the detriment of others. In other words, they believed it failed the "general welfare" test.

Vice President John C. Calhoun of South Carolina vehemently opposed the tariff. In December 1828, he secretly wrote a pamphlet entitled *South Carolina Exposition and Protest* laying out the case against the tariff. He also asserted that a single state had the authority to veto – or nullify in law – an act of the federal government, subject to override only by three-fourths of the states.

> "To the States respectively each in its sovereign capacity is reserved the power, by its veto, or right of interposition, to arrest the encroachment. And, finally, may this power be abused by a State, so as to interfere improperly with the powers delegated to the General Government? There is provided a power, even over the Constitution itself, vested in three fourths of the States, which Congress has the authority to invoke, and may terminate all controversies in reference to the subject, by granting or withholding the right in contest. Its authority is acknowledged by all; and to deny or resist it, would be, on the part of the

State, a violation of the constitutional compact, and a dissolution of the political association, as far as it is concerned. This is the ultimate and highest power, and the basis on which the whole system rests. . . ."

The relationship between President Andrew Jackson and Calhoun deteriorated as the president refused to address southern grievances. In 1832, Calhoun resigned the vice presidency and filled an open seat in the U.S. Senate.

That same year, Congress passed the Tariff of 1832, but it did little to relieve the burden on southern states. In response, South Carolina elected delegates to a special convention, and on November 24, the convention ratified the South Carolina Ordinance of Nullification. The proclamation declared that the tariffs of 1828 and 1832, *"are unauthorized by the constitution of the United States, and violate the true meaning and intent thereof and are null, void, and no law, nor binding upon this State."*

But the Ordinance didn't stop at a simple statement of opinion. It also made clear that South Carolina was intending to take serious measures to prevent any agent – state or federal – from enforcing the Tariff.

> *And it is further ordained, that it shall not be lawful for any of the constituted authorities, whether of this State or of the United States, to enforce the payment of duties imposed by the said acts within the limits of this State; but it shall be the duty of the legislature to adopt such measures and pass such acts as may be necessary to give full effect to this ordinance, and to prevent the enforcement and arrest the operation of the said acts and parts of acts of the Congress of the United States within the limits of this State, from and after the first day of February next, and the duties of all other constituted authorities, and of all persons residing or being within the limits of this State, and they are hereby required and enjoined to obey and give effect to this ordinance, and such acts and measures of the legislature as may be passed or adopted in obedience thereto.*

Madison fundamentally disagreed with South Carolina's position. While he opposed the tariff from a policy standpoint, he believed it was a constitutional exercise of federal power. And, while Madison did advise in *Federalist #46* a "refusal to cooperate with officers of the Union" as a response to both unconstitutional and constitutional federal acts, he held the view that state actions to physically block implementation of federal acts was something reserved for a "deliberate, palpable, and dangerous exercise of other powers."

Quite simply, Madison didn't consider the tariff to be a policy which warranted such a strong response. Because of this, he viewed South Carolina's position as untenable.

3 VIRGINIA'S RESOLUTIONS OF 1798

Supporters of South Carolina's position turned to Madison's *Virginia Resolutions of 1798* to defend their position. In the resolutions, Madison asserted the right of the states, as parties to the Constitution, to declare a federal act unconstitutional and take action when the general government exercised undelegated powers.

> *"That in case of a deliberate, palpable, and dangerous exercise of other powers, not granted by the said compact, the states who are parties thereto, have the right, and are in duty bound, to interpose for arresting the progress of the evil, and for maintaining within their respective limits, the authorities, rights and liberties appertaining to them."*

Keep in mind, the resolutions were just that — resolutions. They were not legally binding and did not, in themselves, authorize Virginia to interpose to stop execution of the *Alien and Sedition Acts.* The resolutions simply asserted the states have the right to:

1. Declare an act unconstitutional.
2. Interpose to stop execution of the act.

Madison expounded on the limited scope of the resolutions when defending them against Federalist Party opponents in the *Report of 1800.*

> "Nor can the declarations of either, whether affirming or denying the constitutionality of measures of the Federal Government, or whether made before or after judicial decisions thereon, be deemed, in any point of view, an assumption of the office of the judge. The declarations, in such cases, are expressions of opinion, unaccompanied with any other effect than what they may produce on opinion, by exciting reflection. The expositions of the judiciary, on the other hand, are carried into immediate effect by force. The former may lead to a change in the legislative expression of the general will; possibly to a change in the opinion of the

judiciary; the latter enforces the general will, whilst that will and that opinion continue unchanged."

Although they articulated important principles, the Virginia Resolutions were **not** a nullification bill. They didn't authorize any state action, but they asserted the principles should the state legislature choose to take further action.

4 CALHOUN'S NULLIFICATION

We must take these important points into consideration when analyzing Madison's *Notes*. Calhoun and others took the principles articulated in the *Virginia Resolutions* and concocted a legal doctrine Madison never contemplated. He was not pleased, and that should be obvious to anyone reading his *Notes*.

More importantly, we need to focus on exactly what Madison was opposing. He was **not** addressing nullification in the abstract, but a bastardized process of nullification concocted by Calhoun and the South Carolina nullifiers. He makes this clear early on:

> *"That the doctrine of nullification may be clearly understood it must be taken as laid*

13

down in the Report of a special committee of the House of Representatives of S. C. in 1828. In that document it is asserted, that a single State has a constitutional right to arrest the execution of a law of the U. S. within its limits; that the arrest is to be presumed right and valid, and is to remain in force unless ¾ of the States, in a Convention, shall otherwise decide."

South Carolina essentially asserted that once a single state nullified a federal act, it was annulled within that state and it could not be legally enforced there until three-quarters of the other states overruled the nullification. Furthermore, South Carolina claimed that a state's act of nullification was "presumed right and valid" until overturned.

In other words, a single state could effectively control the entire country.

Representatives of the Palmetto State forwarded this idea as a "constitutional" remedy. The South Carolina version of nullification held that a single state's action **legally bound** the rest of the country and annulled – or made legally inoperative – the federal act within that state.

It's important to understand that South Carolina was using, and Madison was addressing, a very precise, legal definition of nullification. The modern day nullification movement uses the term in a more practical, Jeffersonian, natural-right sense.

Such a view holds that a federal act is nullified when it is no longer enforced as a result of actions to resist, block, or frustrate its enforcement. Such state action does not legally invalidate the federal law. It does not erase the law from the books. It does not legally compel the federal government to stop enforcing it. It has no *legal* force at the federal level at all. It simply directs the state to refuse cooperation and/or work to hinder implementation of the act within the state. Madison was addressing the South Carolina doctrine that defined nullification in a legal sense – to annul the law – or render it legally invalid, like a veto.

Of course, we find no such mechanism in the Constitution, and Madison rightly argued this idea was absurd.

> "But it follows, from no view of the subject, that a nullification of a law of the U. S. can *as is now contended*, belong rightfully to a single State, as one of the parties to the Constitution; the State not ceasing to avow

its adherence to the Constitution. A plainer contradiction in terms, or a more fatal inlet to anarchy, cannot be imagined." [Emphasis added]

Quite simply, a single state can't bind other political societies – neither the other states, nor the union of states created by the Constitution. A single state has no power to legally require federal agents to cease enforcement of federal acts. No mechanism exists for a single state to veto a federal act and force other states or the federal government to recognize that veto as "right and valid." The Constitution does not establish any such process, as Madison asserted in the *Notes*.

> *"The true question therefore is whether there be a **constitutional** right in a single state to nullify a law of the U. S. We have seen the absurdity of such a claim in its naked and suicidal form."* [Emphasis original]

This was the "nullification" Madison was addressing in his *Notes* – a process dreamed up by Calhoun and South Carolina statesmen - and readers must keep that context in mind.

Modern nullification opponents fail to do so. They ignore what Madison was clearly addressing by taking quotes from *Notes* and using them to attack Jeffersonian nullification, the foundation of the modern nullification movement.

5 JEFFERSON'S NULLIFICATION: A NATURAL RIGHT

So, did Madison ever express opposition to Jeffersonian Nullification as understood in 1798?

Throughout the *Notes*, Madison calls into question a "constitutional right" to nullification.

What did he mean?

Quite simply, he meant that the doctrine of nullification does not exist in the text of the Constitution itself. The framers did not spell it out. Legitimate nullification is not a "constitutional process" as South Carolina claimed. It was not explicitly written into the founding document.

In fact, legitimate nullification is not a mere "parchment barrier," a phrase used in the founding times as something created by the words of document, and not pre or super-ceding it.

Thomas Jefferson first formally articulated the principles in his original draft of the *Kentucky Resolutions of 1798*.

The *Alien and Sedition Acts* outraged many in Kentucky. Several counties in the Commonwealth adopted resolutions condemning the acts, including Fayette, Clark, Bourbon, Madison and Woodford. A Madison County Kentucky militia regiment issued an ominous resolution of its own, stating, "The Alien and Sedition Bills are an infringement of the Constitution and of natural rights, and that we cannot approve or submit to them." Several thousand people gathered at an outdoor meeting protesting the acts in Lexington on August 13, 1798.

The push to nullify the *Alien and Sedition Acts* was not simply the act of opportunistic politicians. It rose out of the passionate demands of the citizenry in Kentucky, as well as Virginia.

Jefferson penned the original draft of *the Kentucky Resolutions* within a month of Congress passing the Sedition Act. First, he made it clear that any federal act not authorized by the Constitution is, by definition, a nullity.

*"That the several States composing, the United States of America, are not united on the principle of unlimited submission to their general government; but that, by a compact under the style and title of a Constitution for the United States, and of amendments thereto, they constituted a general government for special purposes — delegated to that government certain definite powers, reserving, each State to itself, the residuary mass of right to their own self-government; and that whensoever the general government assumes undelegated powers, **its acts are unauthoritative, void, and of no force.**"*
[Emphasis added]

This was no new idea. Jefferson simply affirmed a principle well-established before the ratification of the Constitution. Alexander Hamilton made the same assertion in *Federalist 78.*

"There is no position which depends on clearer principles, than that every act of a delegated authority contrary to the tenor of the commission under which it is exercised, is void. No legislative act, therefore, contrary to the constitution, can be valid."

This same principle was written into law as Article VI of the Constitution, the "Supremacy Clause."

Jefferson then goes on to show that the federal government (i.e. the courts) does not determine the extent of the powers delegate to itself. This is, in fact, an absurdity. You cannot have a limited institution determining the extent of its own limitations. That essentially would make its power limitless.

> *"The government created by this compact was not made the exclusive or final judge of the extent of the powers delegated to itself; since that would have made its discretion, and not the Constitution, the measure of its powers; but that, as in all other cases of compact among powers having no common judge, **each party** has an equal right to judge for itself, as well of infractions as of the mode and measure of redress."*
> [Emphasis added]

It's important to note how Jefferson asserts that **each state** has and equal right to **judge for itself**.

After outlining each constitutional violation and overreach of federal power, Jefferson called for action.

> *"Therefore this commonwealth is determined, as it doubts not its co-States are, to submit to undelegated, and consequently unlimited powers in no man, or body of men on earth: that in cases of an*

*abuse of the delegated powers, the members of the general government, being chosen by the people, a change by the people would be the constitutional remedy; but, where powers are assumed which have not been delegated, **a nullification of the act is the rightful remedy**: that **every State has a natural right in cases not within the compact, (casus non fœderis) to nullify of their own authority all assumptions of power by others within their limits:** that without this right, they would be under the dominion, absolute and unlimited, of whosoever might exercise this right of judgment for them."* [Emphasis added]

Nullification exists as a "natural right" of self-defense against usurpations of power.

Jefferson sent former Virginia ratifying convention delegate Wilson Cary Nicholas a draft of the resolution, likely hoping the state legislator could get them introduced in Virginia. In October, 1798, Wilson indicated that state representative John Breckinridge was willing to introduce the resolutions in Kentucky. Breckinridge suffered from tuberculosis and made a recuperative trip to Sweet Springs, Va. late in August of that year. Nicholas likely gave the Kentucky lawmaker a copy of Jefferson's draft during that trip.

On Nov. 7, 1798, Gov. James Garrard addressed the Kentucky state legislature, noting the vehement opposition to the Alien and Sedition Acts. That same day, Breckinridge announced to the House he intended to submit resolutions addressing Garrard's message. The following day, the Fayette County lawmaker followed through, introducing an amended version of Jefferson's draft.

Most notably, Breckinridge omitted the word nullification from the actual version considered by the Kentucky legislature, seeking to moderate the tone of the resolution. Removal of the nullification reference apparently didn't bother Jefferson, and in fact, did little to change the fundamental thrust of the resolution. By declaring the *Alien and Sedition Acts* **unconstitutional, null and void**, the Kentucky legislature voted on a nullification resolution even with the actual word omitted.

The bill passed the House on Nov. 10 with only three dissenting votes. The Senate unanimously concurred three days later, and Gov. Garrard signed the resolution on Nov. 16.

In the wake of opposition primarily from northern Federalist Party controlled states, Kentucky followed up with a second resolution affirming its position in 1799, notably including the word "nullification," omitted in the final version of the

Kentucky Resolutions of 1798 passed by the state legislature.

> *"The several states who formed that instrument (the Constitution), being sovereign and independent, have the unquestionable right to judge of its infraction; and, That a nullification, by those sovereignties, of all unauthorized acts done under color of that instrument, is the rightful remedy."*

6 MADISON ON JEFFERSON'S NULLIFICATION

Modern day nullification supporters trace their principles directly back to the Jeffersonian conception of the word, not the South Carolina/John Calhoun bastardization of the principles.

So, did Madison reject this Jeffersonian idea in 1835? Absolutely not! Even while arguing against South Carolina nullification, Madison continued to affirm Jeffersonian nullification in his *Notes*.

> "Thus the right of nullification meant by Mr. Jefferson is **the natural right, which all admit to be a remedy against insupportable oppression.** It cannot be supposed for a moment that Mr. Jefferson

> *would not revolt at the doctrine of South Carolina, that a single state could constitutionally resist a law of the Union while remaining within it, and that with the accession of a small minority of the others, overrule the will of a great majority of the whole, & constitutionally annul the law everywhere."* [Emphasis added]

Madison again states his opposition to the specific "doctrine of South Carolina," the bastardized version of nullification created by Calhoun. He also emphatically asserts that "all admit" nullification to be a "natural right" - a legitimate and valid option to stop the oppression of federal usurpation.

In other words, when the federal government unchains itself from its constitutional restraint, the people of the states have the right to defend themselves and stop it.

> *"The provision made by a Constn. for its own exposition, thro' its own authorities & forms, must prevail whilst the Constitution is left to itself by those who made it; or until cases arise which **justify a resort to ultra-constitutional interpositions."** [Emphasis added]*

Jefferson and Madison differed strategically on when nullification should be employed. Jefferson supported its use "whensoever" the federal government acted beyond the Constitution, and Madison supported its use as a remedy against "insupportable oppression." But both took the position that nullification was power far greater than a process created by words on paper.

Nearly all the founders believed in a natural law and rights theory of the sort outlined by political philosopher John Locke and incorporated in the Declaration of Independence. While a government or legal system bestows legal rights upon a person, natural rights are not contingent upon anything of the sort. They exist by virtue of personhood, and therefore stand as universal and inalienable.

By referring to nullification as a natural right, both Jefferson and Madison considered it something that could neither be given, nor taken away by any government or legal system.

Madison never abandoned this position and reaffirmed it in his *Notes on Nullification*:

> *"Under these circumstances, the subject was taken up by Virga. in her resolutions, and pursued at the ensuing session of the Legislature in a comment explaining and justifying them; her main and immediate object, evidently being, to produce a conviction everywhere, that the Constitution had been*

violated by the obnoxious acts and to procure a concurrence and co-operation of the other States in effectuating a repeal of the acts. She accordingly asserted and offered her proofs at great length, that the acts were unconstitutional. She asserted moreover & offered her proofs that the States had a right in such cases, to interpose, first in their constituent character to which the govt of the U. S. was responsible, and otherwise as specially provided by the Constitution; and further, that the States, in their capacity of parties to and creators of the Constitution, had an ulterior right to interpose, notwithstanding any decision of a constituted authority; which, however it might be the last resort under the forms of the Constitution in cases falling within the scope of its functions, could not preclude an interposition of the States as the parties which made the Constitution and, as such, possessed an authority paramount to it."

7 CONSTITUTIONAL FOUNDATION

To consider nullification an "ultra-constitutional" constitutional process is not to say it is "unconstitutional" or illegal. In fact, the principle fits perfectly into America's constitutional system.

Nullification follows from a constitutional delegation of power. The people first created independent, sovereign political societies – States – and delegated powers to their state governments. Then, the people, through those preexisting political societies, delegated specific, enumerated powers to a general government in order to form a union.

By delegating a limited set of power, it logically follows that the framers intended to exclude all others from the federal government. *Designato unius est exclusio alterius* – a legal maxim meaning, "the designation of one is the exclusion of the other."

For example, some argue that the term "general welfare" implies a more sweeping delegation of power. Madison emphatically said that it does not in *Federalist 41*.

> *"Had no other enumeration or definition of the powers of the Congress been found in the Constitution, than the general expressions just cited, the authors of the objection might have had some color for it; though it would have been difficult to find a reason for so awkward a form of describing an authority to legislate in all possible cases. A power to destroy the freedom of the press, the trial by jury, or even to regulate the course of descents, or the forms of conveyances, must be very singularly expressed by the terms 'to raise money for the general welfare.'*

> *"But what color can the objection have, when a specification of the objects alluded to by these general terms immediately follows, and is not even separated by a longer pause than a semicolon?...For what purpose could the enumeration of particular powers be inserted, if these and all others were meant to be included in the preceding*

> *general power? Nothing is more natural nor common than first to use a general phrase, and then to explain and qualify it by a recital of particulars."*

Many opponents of ratification remained unconvinced and insisted on amendments "in order to prevent misconstruction or abuse of [the federal government's] powers." This led to the Bill of Rights.

Here, in the Ninth and Tenth Amendments, we find the constitutional basis for nullification.

These two amendments are known as "rules of construction." They don't delegate any new federal power; they simply work together to explain the proper reading and interpretation of the entire document.

The Tenth Amendment clarifies the extent of federal power, making it explicit that the federal government may only exercise the powers enumerated.

*"The powers **not delegated** to the United States by the Constitution, **nor prohibited by it to the States**, are reserved to the States respectively, or to the people. "* [Emphasis added]

In light of the Tenth Amendment, we must ask two questions when it comes to nullification.

1. Does the Constitution delegate any such power to the federal government? Clearly not.
2. Does the Constitution explicitly prohibit nullification? Again, it does not.

Therefore, it follows that nullification remains a legitimate power reserved to the states and the people.

The Ninth Amendment provides an even clearer justification for nullification.

Many feared that listing certain protected rights in a Bill of Rights would lead people to believe that the federal government could violate other rights not listed. Madison addressed this fear in his speech to Congress on the day he proposed the Bill of Rights.

> *"It has been objected also against a Bill of Rights, that, by enumerating particular exceptions to the grant of power, it would disparage those rights which were not placed in that enumeration; and it might follow by implication, that those rights which were not singled out, were intended to be assigned into the hands of the General Government, and were consequently insecure. This is one of the most plausible arguments I have ever heard against the admission of a bill of rights into this system; but, I conceive, that it may be guarded*

against. I have attempted it, as gentlemen may see by turning to the last clause of the fourth resolution."

Madison's last clause of the fourth resolution read as follows.

"The exceptions here or elsewhere in the constitution, made in favor of particular rights, shall not be so construed as to diminish the just importance of other rights retained by the people; or as to enlarge the powers delegated by the constitution; but either as actual limitations of such powers, or as inserted merely for greater caution."

This eventually became the Ninth Amendment.

"The enumeration in the Constitution, of certain rights, shall not be construed to deny or disparage others retained by the people."

Remember, Jefferson described nullification as a natural right, and Madison reaffirmed the validity of Jeffersonian, natural-right nullification in his *Notes*. Nullification is a natural right of self-defense when the federal government violates the highest law of the land. Since the Constitution does not specifically prohibit nullification, the federal government has no authority to interfere with it. It remains a valid right to be exercised by the people of the states when they determine it necessary for their protection.

Quite simply, per the Ninth Amendment, the federal government may not "deny or disparage" the natural right of nullification.

In his *Notes*, Madison pointed out that the right of nullification exists in all political societies, including the United States.

> *"Should the constituted authorities of the State unite in usurping oppressive powers; should the constituent Body fail to arrest the progress of the evil thro' the elective process according to the forms of the Constitution; and should the authority which is above that of the Constitution, the majority of the people, inflexibly support the oppression inflicted on the minority, nothing would remain for the minority, but **to rally to its reserved rights** (for **every citizen has his reserved rights**, as exemplified in Declarations prefixed to most of the State constitutions), and to decide between acquiescence & resistance, according to the calculation above stated."*

According to Madison, nullification stands as the last resort to stop the federal government. To deny that right means complete submission, clearly something never contemplated by the Madison or the other Founders.

8 PRE-CONSTITUTIONAL ROOTS

Madison actually provided the blueprint for
nullification in a practical sense before the
Constitution was even ratified. In *Federalist #46*, he
specifically answers the question: how do the
people stop the federal government from
exercising undelegated power?

*"Should an unwarrantable measure of the federal
government be unpopular in particular States,
which would seldom fail to be the case, or even a
warrantable measure be so, which may sometimes
be the case, the means of opposition to it are
powerful and at hand. The disquietude of the
people; their repugnance and, perhaps **refusal to
cooperate with officers of the Union**, the frowns of*

*the executive magistracy of the State; the embarrassment created by **legislative devices**, which would often be added on such occasions, would oppose, in any State, **very serious impediments**; and were the sentiments of several adjoining States happen to be in Union, would **present obstructions** which the federal government would hardly be willing to encounter."* [Emphasis added]

Let's break down Madison's prescription.

"Should an unwarrantable measure..." What does Madison mean by "unwarrantable?" The word literally means "unjustifiable." Madison was clearly talking about federal acts with no constitutional justification. In other words, unconstitutional.

But notice something interesting, Madison implies that state governments can even resist a "warrantable" or justifiable federal act.

So what does Madison suggest states do when the feds overstep their authority?

Oppose it!

"...the means of opposition to it are powerful and at hand." Madison anticipated the possibility of federal usurpation and clearly believed the states would serve as a check on federal power. He believed the states should and would resist unconstitutional acts.

So, what are the "means of opposition?"

1. Disquietude of the people – This would include protests and petitions generated at the grassroots level. Madison expected the people would throw a fit when the feds usurped power – even using the word "repugnance" to describe their displeasure. That's a pretty strong word. And inevitably, disquietude leads to action – first at the local level, then bubbling up to the state level. That leads to the next step.

2. Refusal to co-operate with the officers of the Union - Noncompliance. The feds rely on cooperation from state and local governments, as well as individuals, to implement and execute their laws. When enough people refuse to comply, they simply can't enforce their so-called laws.

3. The frowns of the executive magistracy of the State - Here Madison envisioned governors formally protesting federal actions. This not only raises public awareness; executive leadership will also lead to the next step – legislative action. Prior to passage of the *Kentucky Resolutions of 1798*,

Gov. Garrard delivered a powerful message condemning the Alien and Sedition Acts and calling on legislative action.

4. Legislative devices, which would often be added on such occasions -What exactly does Madison mean by "legislative devices?" He didn't make that clear in *Federalist #46.* But we know they include resolutions, because he and Jefferson penned the *Kentucky and Virginia Resolutions.*

But do legislative devices stop at non-binding resolutions? Clearly not, because Madison said these measures would create "difficulties" and "impediments." Seventeenth century dictionaries list "obstruction" as a synonym for impediment. In other words, these legislative devices would serve to block the operation of unconstitutional power.

Taken together, this infers state legislative actions including formal, binding prohibitions of state or local cooperation, and outright interposition: "to intervene or place an agency between two positions."

The personal liberty laws passed by northern states to thwart the Fugitive Slave Act of 1850 serve as the best historical example of "legislative devices."

Madison said these actions would be effective as well. They would,

"oppose, in any State, difficulties not to be despised; would form, in a large State, very serious impediments; and where the sentiments of several adjoining States happened to be in unison, would present obstructions which the federal government would hardly be willing to encounter."

9 CONCLUSION

This is an example of what we mean by nullification. Not some legal fiction like South Carolina pulled out of thin air that somehow operates on other states and the federal government itself. We mean nullification as an action taken by a state to render an unconstitutional federal act unenforceable within its borders. It is an exercise of a natural right to stop federal usurpation.

Madison gave us the blueprint. Jefferson formalized the principles. And Madison reaffirmed them in his *Notes on Nullification*, even while railing against the South Carolina version.

When the federal government acts outside of its delegated powers, that act is, by definition, null, void and of no force. The "Supremacy Clause" says as much.

But simply saying so means and does nothing in practice.

Nullifying – "making the act of no value or consequence" - requires action. The operation of the illegal act must be met with acts which result in their lack of enforcement. Nullification is a mechanism to achieve that end, and the people of the states have that right.

Nullification is a natural right of self-defense. It is universal and inalienable.

ABOUT THE AUTHOR

MICHAEL MAHARREY is the national communications director for the Tenth Amendment Center. A long-time journalist by day and hockey player by night, Maharrey earned a B.A. in Mass Communications and Media Studies with an emphasis in news and editorial journalism at the University of South Florida St. Petersburg in 2008.

He covered state and local politics for several newspapers, including the St. Petersburg Times and the Kentucky Gazette. Mike lives in Lexington, Ky. and is working with his wife Cynthia to raise three teenagers.

Made in the USA
San Bernardino, CA
16 November 2017